AIRData 3

US Marine Corps Harrier

1 – Harrier Origins	4	
2 – The AV-8B	6	
3 – AV-8B(NA) Night Attack	18	
4 – Harrier Walkaround	28	
5 – AV-8B Harrier II Plus	44	
6 – TAV-8B	60	
Colour Profiles	57	
Appendix I AV-8B Squadrons	65	
Appendix II AV-8B Specifications	66	

First produced in 2009 by SAM Limited, under licence from SAM Publications
Media House, 21 Kingsway, Bedford, MK42 9BJ, United Kingdom

© 2009 SAM Publications
© Andy Evans – Text
© Andy Evans – Colour artwork

All rights reserved. No part of this publication may be reproduced or transmitted in any form or by any means, electronic or mechanical, including photocopy, recording, or any other information storage and retrieval system, without permission in writing from the publishers.

ISBN 978-1-906959-06-7

Typeset by SAM Limited, Media House, 21 Kingsway, Bedford, MK42 9BJ, UK
Designed by Simon Sugarhood
Printed and bound in the United Kingdom by Symbian Print Intelligence Ltd

Author's Note
Whilst every care has been taken in the gathering of images for this book, either from original sources, via third party collections or the author's own archives, every effort has been made to identify and credit photographers responsible for the photograph and where possible obtain the necessary permissions for their use. However the publishers cannot accept responsibility for any omissions beyond their control and should any persons feel their copyright has been inadvertently breached, please contact the author via the publisher.

Acknowledgments
Thanks are due to the following for their assistance with information and photographs that populate this publication:
BAe Systems Press Office, McDonnell Douglas (Boeing) Press Office, US Navy Public Affairs, US Marine Corps Public Affairs, Captain Mike Richardson USMC and Mark Smith.

Andy Evans
July 2009

Chapter 1
AV-8B Origins

⇧ The original AV-8A, based on the RAF Harrier GR.1, was a major success story in Marines manoeuvre warfare

The operational success of the earlier AV-8A/C had confirmed the US Marine Corps' belief in VSTOL technology and its advantages for their particular type of warfare. What was needed now was a follow-on aircraft that met the Corps' future requirements for a 'light attack' aircraft that carried a big punch. The unique Harrier, previously much maligned by the US military as 'not being able to carry a matchbox across a football field' had matured into a very capable aircraft which the US Marine Corps saw as a highly valued asset. The need for a new generation of VSTOL galvanised studies undertaken by McDonnell Douglas, following their abortive collaborative AV-16 'Advanced Harrier' effort with the UK. These studies came under the aegis of the AV-8A Plus, a much less ambitious programme than the AV-16, which delighted the Marines who wanted the Harrier to be simple and survivable. In turn this became the AV-8B Program, which was originally proposed in 1973 and formalised by the

⇧ Following on from the AV-8A came the upgraded AV-8C

⇧ The latest incarnation of the ubiquitous Harrier family is the radar-equipped Harrier II Plus

Defence Armed Services Committee in March 1976.

Central to this new breed of Harrier was an advanced 'big-wing', originally proposed by Hawker and later derived from NASA-based technology of supercritical aerofoils, where the drag was reduced and the lift increased. To achieve the maximum benefits in terms of weight saving, advanced structural materials were used instead of traditional metal, and a unique graphite epoxy construction gave the AV-8B the first carbon-fibre technology wing fitted to a military aircraft. At the rear of the wing a large, single-slotted flap was integrated to support the jet efflux from the engine nozzles, which increased take-off lift and helped to arrest the loss of performance during vertical landings. The cockpit would be raised and the outrigger wheels moved inboard the better to facilitate rough field work, and the `elephant's ear' engine intakes were also redesigned and increased in size, initially with a double row of 'blow-in' suction relief doors (later revised to a single row) and reshaped forward cold-air nozzles with a `zero-scarf' design; these two features alone added an amazing 800lb of thrust.

⇧ The AV-8B was an entirely new animal and packed a mighty punch

⇧ An AV-8B(NA) Night Attack Harrier comes in to land

Chapter 2
The AV-8B

⇧ Here you get a great view of the Harrier's 'big wing'

Part of the original Phase I of the 1976 Advanced Harrier Program was the production of two Harrier Technology Demonstrators, as well as a full-scale wind tunnel test with the use of AV-8A 158385; this was successfully completed in late 1976. The primary element of Phase 11 of the Program was to test the theories behind the AV-8B in a flight programme and to accommodate this two AV-8As were remanufactured as YAV-8B test aircraft. YAV-8B No.1, 158394, was completed on 1 September 1978, with its first flight on 9 November, and the second, YAV-8B, 158395, flew on 19 February 1979. Modifications to these aircraft incorporated the new supercritical wing, improved inlet system and positive circulation flaps. The engine was the Pegasus 11 F402-RR-404 with 21,700lb of thrust, which included a new gearbox and zero-scarf forward nozzles and the same Lift Improvement Devices that were added to the AV-8C. The main fuselage of the aircraft remained largely unchanged from the standard AV-8A and included the under-fuselage Aden gun packs with strakes. McDonnell Douglas also produced a full-scale mock-up 159234/20 to show what the AV-8B might look like, using parts from a crashed AV-8A with the new wing; this too still used the basic Harrier I fuselage. The trials were impressive, going through the full extent of the flight envelope and weapons capacity; there was no doubt that the AV-8B would provide the much needed improvements in warload and radius of operation that the Marines required. YAV-8B No.1 was deployed aboard USS Saipan for seagoing trials in October 1979 together with the development version of the AV-8C. The promise of the next generation was huge in terms of performance and payload, and with the latest state-of-the-art avionics the US Congress

⇧ The Harrier can carry an unerring array of weaponry compared to the earlier AV-8A/C

⇧ How many Harriers?

⇑ Carrying both defensive and offensive weaponry, a Harrier from VMA-513 rolls in to target

⇑ The ability to operate fixed-wing airpower from unprepared or austere sites remains a major asset for the US Marine Corps

⇧ YAV-8B 158395 flew on 19 February 1979

⇧ Clad in HTPS (Harrier Tactical Paint) colours a rather scruffy 164152/KD Harrier from VMAT-203

ordered four Full Scale Development (FSD) Aircraft, under the full designation AV-8B. Following the completion of the test programme YAV-8B No.1 joined the NASA Test Fleet as N704NA.

Following on from the two YAV-8Bs and the FSD aircraft came an initial batch of twelve production AV-8Bs and a limited run of a further twenty-one. The first of the FSDs, 161396, made its first tentative hover flight on 5 November1981. The AV-8B was a totally changed aircraft compared with the YAV-8. McDonnell Douglas produced the first batches of aircraft in St. Louis, before a work-share agreement with British Aerospace came on line. BAe were responsible for the centre and rear fuselage sections, the fin and rudder, the centreline pylon and the reaction control system, and Rolls-Royce had the very important role of supplying the Pegasus engine. The wing was by now well refined with the LERX (leading edge root extension) added

⇧ Carrying a load of 'Snakeye' bombs, the YAV-8B looks resplendent in its red, white and blue scheme

⇧ One of the 'Tigers' of VMA-542 drops a stick of bombs on one of the practice ranges

to the roots and a completely new tailplane fitted, again using carbon fibre technology. The forward fuselage also used carbon fibre components and, benefiting from the Sea Harrier's experience, enjoyed a redesigned and raised 'bubble' canopy with a wraparound windshield, lifting the crew position by 10.5in, thereby giving a much better view and providing room below for the some of the new avionics. The ejector seat fitted was the UPC/Stencel 10B, with zero-zero capabilities.

The avionics themselves were in the main brand new, although some were unashamedly borrowed from other McDonnell Douglas programmes. In the nose was a Hughes ARBS (Angle-Rate Bombing System), originally developed for the A-4M Skyhawk, with a TV and dual-mode tracker facility, projecting its information on to a Smiths Industries upgraded SU-128/A HUD or on to the MFD (multi-function display) in the cockpit on the pilot's left, on which could be shown sensor information, nav/mission plots, ARN-118 TACAN information and engine data, and the SAAHS (stability augmentation and attitude-hold system). Such systems assist the accurate delivery of laser-guided as well as 'dumb' bombs. Some of the cockpit interfaces were borrowed from the F-18: items such as the improved HOTAS (Hands-On-Throttle-And-Stick) controls, the AYK-14 mission computer, the ASN-130 INS, the Lear Siegler AN/AYQ-13 stores management system, and the ECM-resistant fibre optic cables. The RWR and underfuselage AN/ALE-39 chaff and flare dispensers were the same as those used in the AV-8C programme. All the aircraft information was fed through a 1553A databus. Also fitted was a Sperry Auto Pilot and

⇧ A veritable 'patchwork' of colours is evident on this VMAT-203 AV-8B!

⇧ A trio of 'Bumblebees' from VMA-331

⇧ Note the removable In Flight Refuelling probe on the engine intake

⇧ Armed with two 'Rockeye' CBU's an AV-8B taxies out at 29 Palms

⇧ Two AV-8As were remanufactured as YAV-8B test aircraft. YAV-8B No.1 158394 seen here was completed on 1 September 1978

⇧ Note the protective caps on the ARBS and pitot tubes

⇧ An AV-8B gets in check before take-off from MCAS Cherry Point

⇧ An AV-8B from VMA-542, with their familiar 'tiger tail', prepares to take-off from a Marines Assault Ship

⇧ 161584/KD of VMAT-203 – note the camouflage on the leading edge of the pylons

⇧ Note here how the wraparound camouflage extends over the underfuselage gun pods on this 'Bulldogs' machine

⇧ A VMA-331 aircraft taxies out

⇧ With flight gear hanging on the weapons pylons this AV-8B from VMA-231 'Ace of Spades' awaits its call to duty

⇧ A VMAT-203 Harrier in grey/green wraparound camouflage taxies in

⇧ 161584/KD of VMAT-203

communications were provided by two ARC-182 wide band UHF/VHF radios, and the ECM suite included the highly efficient AN/ALR-67 RWR system. The entire cockpit was of a more ergonomically satisfactory design than the 'ergonomic slum' of previous Harriers. To add more muscle to its attack potential a new gun, the General Electric GAU-12A Equaliser, was developed and fitted with strakes for better LID effect. The gun was housed in a left-hand underfuselage pod, with 300 rounds of ammunition held in a right-hand pod, fed to the gun via a bridge across the underfuselage. The gun was able to discharge 3,600rpm, driven by bleed air from the engine.

The four FSDs, the twelve 'initial production' and the twenty-one 'limited production' aircraft were fitted with an interim F402-RR-404A engine, before the production batch proper were fitted with the definitive F404-RR-406, with

⇧ With its IFR probe extended an AV-8B takes on gas

⇧ An AV-8B demonstrates its 'in field-operations' ability

⇧ A classic shot of a VMA-331 Harrier in green and grey camouflage speeding toward its target

zero-scarfed front nozzles and the DECS engine controls. The first aircraft that would bear the name 'Harrier II' FSD.1 was officially rolled out on 16 October 1981 and used to undertake the initial hovering trials and the basic flight characteristics tests. This aircraft was not fitted with the LERX and still carried the YAV-8B style double row of intake doors. The second aircraft, FSD.2, 161397, was the first to be fitted with the new 'bolt-on' retractable IFR probe, and undertook aerial tanking trials. This aircraft also introduced the LERX and the single row of blow-in doors on the engine intakes. FSD.3, 161398, undertook avionics and weapons trials, while FSD.4, 161399, which flew in June 1983 was as near to a 'production' AV-8B as possible. The aircraft were based out of Patuxent River as part of VX-5.

VMAT-203 received its first AV-8B in a ceremony on 12 January 1984, when it was officially handed 161573/KD-21. VMAT203 was given most of the early production models for pilot training and conversion at MCAS Cherry Point. VMA-331, 'The Bumblebees', was the first unit of the front-line 'gun squadrons' to get its hands on the AV-8B, followed at Cherry Point by VMA-231, VMA-223 and VMA-542, while at Yuma VMA-513, stood down the Marines' last AV-8C in August 1986 for the AV-8B; VMA-211 and VMA311 also traded-up for the Harrier II. Thus far only one Harrier unit has been stood down in consequence of the post-Cold War cutbacks: the AV-8Bs of VMA-311 were decommissioned in October 1992.

⇧ One of the early AV-8B's assigned to VMAT-203 wearing the original three-tone colour scheme

⇧ The first of the FSDs, 161396. Note the instrumentation boom and the lack of the LERX at the wing root

⇧ In the nose of the AV-8B is the Hughes ARBS (Angle-Rate Bombing System)

⇧ Ready to roll!

⇧ Note here the huge flaps extended as this AV-8 gets airborne. Note also the wraparound two-tone camouflage

⇧ The aftermath of war as an AV-8B passes Kuwait's burning oilfields

AV-8B goes to War

On the 2 August 1990, Iraq invaded Kuwait, and this was the start of a campaign that would pit the AV-8B Harrier II of the US Marine Corps in combat for the first time. The first Marine Corps tactical aviation to arrive in theatre were the AV-8Bs which were to be tasked with providing their own brand of CAS (close air support). When the invasion of Kuwait occurred, the last two of the MCAS Yuma-based Harrier units were in the middle of converting from their 'vanilla' AV-8Bs to the new night-attack Harrier. Those aircraft scheduled for deployment were repainted in a two-tone, grey camouflage scheme, more suited to the desert skyline. On 18 and 19 August Yuma-based VMA-311, 'The Bumblebees', and Cherry Point-based VMA-542, (swapping some of their jets for the DECS-equipped aircraft from VMAT203) headed out across the Atlantic; refuelling at night from USAF KC-10s they were soon ready for their part in Operation Desert Shield.

After a short stay in Bahrain, VMA-311 moved to King Abdul Aziz Air Base (KAAAB), ideally situated, being just 100 miles from the Kuwaiti border. Once facilities had been established, the 'Flying Tigers' also made the move from

⇧ Rows of 'iron bombs' wait beside a 'Rockeye' armed Harrier

Bahrain to KAAAB in November. Also by mid-August VMA-331 had arrived and deployed aboard the assault ship USS Nassau. A second wave of twenty Harriers arrived from VMA-231, having been on deployment at Iwakuni in Japan To the north the Marines had established a FARP (Forward Area Rearm/Refuel Point) at an Aramco helicopter base at Tanajib, from where the aircraft could refuel and rearm, and, because it was only 5 min flight time from the border, this

⇧ On the ground at King Abdul Aziz, AV-8B 163201 is seen armed with 'fire bombs'. Note the 'dual identity' of VMA-223 and VMA-542

⇧ Back at MCAS Cherry Point this aircraft from VMA-223 still wears its 'war-paint'

⇧ Jump-jet-jockey's! A pair of Harrier flyers pose with their survival gear

⇧ 162964 in a lighter version of the Gulf camouflage, seen post-war at MCAS Cherry Point

⇧ The Hughes ARBS (Angle Rate Bombing System) proved very effective in the war

⇧ 163195 post-war at MCAS Cherry Point, looking well worn. Note the painted-over number on the nose

meant that the Harriers could provide a rapid response to any call for assistance.

The first action for the Harriers came when in support of a Marines position which was under attack near the border town of Khafji. Four VMA-311 aircraft on alert were launched, followed swiftly by VMA-542 and VMA-231, and these jets successfully attacked and silenced the guns with 1,000lb bombs and cannon fire. From then on the Harriers carried forward their attacks on Iraqi elements right up until a cease-fire was eventually called on 28 February.

⇧ Armed with six 'Rockeye' CBU's a VMA-542 Harrier heads for its target area

Chapter 3
AV-8B(NA) Night Attack

⇧ Showing its dedicated nose artwork, and array of weaponry and a very 'sooty' cannon, 162966 conducts air-trials

The ability to operate their Harriers 'after dark' was of great importance to US Marine Corps philosophy, and the retirement of the A-6 Intruder left quite a capability gap. Its interest in a nocturnal Harrier-based capability was enhanced by Forward Looking Infra-Red (FLIR) trials being carried out at China Lake, where a TA-7C Corsair was fitted with a pod-mounted system, complemented with pilot NVG's and a night compatible cockpit. A 'proof of concept' aircraft, AV-8B 162966, complete with night-attack suite, was produced and fitted with a GEC Sensors FLIR, mounted in front of the cockpit, atop the nose section and above and

⇧ Carrying Maverick Missiles and slick bombs the development AV-8B(NA)

⇧ A pair of VMA-211 'Wake Island Avengers' Harriers show off their steeds

⇧ With 'plane guard' in place an AV-8A(NA) prepares to launch

⇧ A dramatic shot of an 'Avengers' Harrier

⇧ Double-trouble! Night Attack and radar-equipped Harriers – a deadly combination!

20

⇧ A good view of the changed nose profile of the AV-8B(NA) with the addition of the FLIR housing

⇧ A mix of Harriers carrying the codes of HMM-261

⇧ 164128 from the 'Wake Island Avengers' taxies out

⇧ Night Attack Harriers such as these took part in Operation Deny Flight over the former Yugoslavia

to the rear of the Hughes AN/ASB-19 Angle Rate Bombing System (ARBS), and within near direct line-of-sight for the pilot. Trials were then undertaken in its new guise after its first flight on 26 June 1987. After successful examination, a production programme was introduced to deliver a new version of the Harrier based on the systems included in the development aircraft.

The first production aircraft to be completed was 163853 which was first flown on 8 July 1989 and delivered into squadron service on 15 September of that year. Originally the aircraft type was to be designated the AV-8D; however AV-8B(NA) became its official nonclementure. The AV-8B(NA) carries modifications that improve its capability and

⇧ Note here the subtle contours of the FLIR housing

⇧ 164121 in the markings of VX-9 'Vampires'

⇧ The AV-8B(NA) is currently operational over the skies of Afghanistan

⇧ An AV-8B(NA) armed with Maverick missile and Rafael Litening II pod

⇧ Note how the upper camouflage has been extended over the rear of the IFR probe

⇧ Perhaps a trick of the light, but this Harrier seems to have a wraparound camouflage scheme as it prepares to launch for an armed patrol over Iraq

survivability, some of which went on to equip the radar-equipped Harrier II Plus. In addition to the FLIR, which gives a 22-degrees field of view, is a Smiths Industries wide-angle HUD and cockpit lighting compatible with the GEC Cat's Eyes NVG's. Also included were upward and downward firing AN/ALE-39 chaff and flare dispensers, the upward firing ones being scabbed on to the topsides of the rear fuselage (an unusual concept for American aircraft, but found on Russian subjects such as the MiG-29 and the Su-27) fitted perhaps in the light of the Soviet experience in Afghanistan. As one US Marine pilot explained, 'Good decoys are vital to us – because of the position of the Harrier's engine exhaust any SAM exploding in close proximity will at the very least take the wing off - a direct hit is something else!' Other improvements saw the introduction of a Honeywell digital moving map display,

⇧ In addition to the nose mounted FLIR the cockpit of the AV-8B(NA) is also NVG compatible

⇧ Note here the mix of ordnance carried by these two aircraft

⇧ A pair of VMA-542 Harriers aboard the USS Nassau. Marines units fly a mix of Night Attack and radar-equipped Harriers

⇧ Looking down on the nose section, showing the upper contours of the FLIR

⇧ The huge air intake of the Harrier is evident in this shot of an AV-8B(NA) as it cushions in to land

⇧ A superb study of the AV-8B(NA) of VMA-513 in its HTPS colours

⇧ The upward firing chaff and flare dispensers scabbed onto the upper rear fuselage

⇧ Heavily armed, the Harriers played a full role in 'Operation Iraqi Freedom'

something deleted from the original AV-8A concept, fed by laser CD and able to be controlled by HOTAS `switchery'. Also included was the `100 per cent LERX' at the wing roots, which was also a retro-fit on converted AV-8A machines. From March 1990 the production standard of the Night Attack Harrier was also raised by the fitting of the Rolls-Royce F402-RR408 11-61 engine, the first aircraft to receive the new powerplant being 163873.

The majority of Night Attack Harriers were to be found at MCAS Yuma in Arizona, and the first unit to take on charge the new breed was VMA-214, 'The Black Sheep', on 1 September 1989, which took its new mounts on deployment to Iwakuni in October 1991. Hot on the heels of 'The Black Sheep' came VMA-211, 'The Wake Island Avengers', which

⇧ 'Everything down' as this AV-8B(NA) come in to land

⇧ Nice teeth!

⇧ The cockpit is night compatible and the pilot wears GEC Cat's Eyes NVG's

⇧ A Night Attack Harrier arrives in the Afghan war zone

⇧ Note the ACMI pod on the starboard wing pylon

⇧ The late evening sun catches this 'Avenger' on its return from patrol over Iraq

converted straight to the Night Attack Harrier from its A-4Ms in spring 1990. It was followed by VMA-311, 'The Tomcats', which traded up its 'vanilla 'AV-8Bs for the AV-8B(NA) in May 1992, and VMA-513, 'The Flying Nightmares', also traded up in September1992. VMA-233 was the only Cherry Point unit to have the Night Attack model from 1992 until converting to the Harrier II Plus in June 1994. The 'Night Attack' Harriers have been involved in all conflicts since 'Operation Desert Storm' and Marines units now operate a 'mix' of AV-8A(NA) aircraft and Harrier II Plus in their squadrons. The Night Attack aircraft continue to provide close air support in both the Iraq and Afghanistan theatres of operation.

⇧ A 'Wake Island Avengers' bird hovers for a landing. Note the squadron insignia on the wing tank

⇧ An AV-8B(NA) makes a smoky landing aboard the USS Tarawa

⇧ Looking down on a Night Attack Harrier as it prepares to launch

Chapter 4
Harrier Walkaround

⇧ The original nose profile of the AV-8B

⇧ The AV-8B Harrier II Plus brought a radome and revised FLIR housing

⇧ The AV-8B(NA) Night Attack variant added a FLIR

⇧ Nose-on contours of the AV-8B Harrier II Plus

⇧ The compact APG-65 radar system

⇧ Nose-on contours of the AV-8B(NA) Night Attack Harrier

⇧ The APG-65 radar as used in the F/A-18 Hornet

⇧ The 'bubble' canopy affords the pilot much better vision

⇧ Close-up on the canopy and the headrest of the Stencil seat

⇧ Blow-in doors and IFR probe

⇧ The bolt-on IFR probe

⇧ 100% LERX and engine fire access port

⇧ Close-in on the head of the IFR probe

⇧ Zero-scarf forward engine nozzle

⇧ Wing edge 'puffer' duct

⇧ Nosewheel doors

⇧ Looking down the rear 'hot' nozzle

⇧ Detail of the nosewheel leg

⇧ LID (Lift Improvement Device) 'dam' forward of the gunpack/strakes

*AIR*Data 31

⇧ Wing pylon detail and wing fence

⇧ Looking upward at the position of the rear 'hot' nozzle

⇧ Close-up on the outrigger wheel tyre

⇧ Outrigger wheel from the rear aspect   ⇧ Main wheels in detail

⇧ The port side of the 'Equaliser' cannon pack containing the gun element

⇧ The tails of the AV-8B(NA) and II Plus have a ram air extension at the root of the fin

⇧ Tailcone detail showing ECM blisters

⇧ Anti-collision light and GPS aerial

⇧ Chaff and flare dispensers scabbed to the AV-8B(NA) and II Plus

⇧ Fully loaded chaff and flare dispensers

⇧ Rear fuselage and wing detail from rear aspect

⇧ Rear 'hot' nozzle in detail

⇧ Airbrake

⇧ A good view of the 'burning' on the paintwork behind the rear nozzle

⇧ The starboard side of the 'Equaliser' cannon pack containing the ammunition

⇧ Main wheels from the starboard aspect

⇧ The nosewheel leg and tyre from the starboard aspect

⇧ Pylon sway brace

⇧ Starboard side cold nozzle and vents, sometimes confused with aerials

⇧ Wing flap line

⇧ Formation lights on the wingtips

⇧ Wing pylon and intake detail

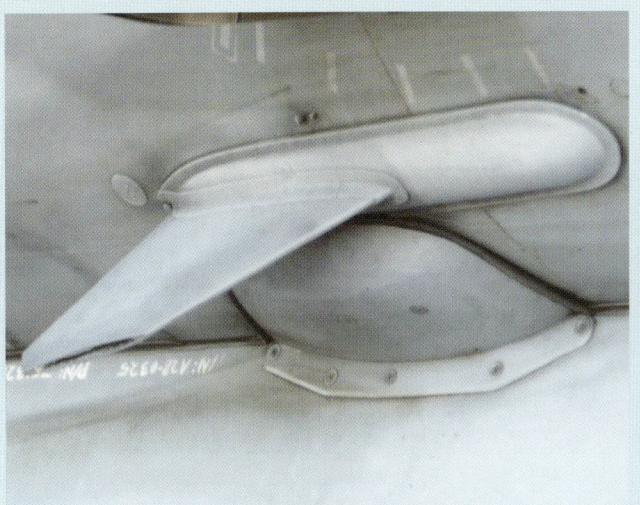
⇧ Oil pressure vent

⇧ Looking down the intake onto the vanes of the Pegasus engine. Note the white interior

⇧ Pull-down pilot's access step

⇧ Nosewheel and LID dam

⇧ Yaw vane

⇧ Engine fire access port

AIRData 37

⇧ Starboard side of the nose. Note the integral steps

⇧ The AV-8B Harrier II Plus cockpit

38

Litening II Pod
Walkaround

⇧ The optics windows of the Litening II pod

⇧ The pod fixed to the pylon

⇧ Underside view

AIRData　39

Harriers in Maintenance
during 'Operation Iraqi Freedom'

⇧ A strange sight – a see-though Harrier!

⇧ One of the 'Blacksheep' wings off, engine out!

⇧ Note the hydraulic jacks holding the aircraft up

⇧ Replacement engine and removed wing

⇧ A Harrier with panels open gets some attention in the field

⇧ The Pegasus engine is removed by crane

Weaponry
Walkaround

⇧ Loading a GBU-38 Joint Attack Direct Munition

⇧ GBU-12's are strapped on

⇧ Crewmen load a GBU-38 Joint Attack Direct Munition

⇧ Paveway III laser guided bombs

⇧ Raising ordnance to the pylons

⇧ A sailor aboard the amphibious assault ship USS Wasp transports Mk82 500 pound bombs across the flight deck

⇧ SUU-25 Flare Pods

AIRData 43

Chapter 5
AV-8B Harrier II Plus

⇧ Here you can see the revised nose of the II Plus with its enlarged radome and angular FLIR. Note also the 100% LERX

The original concept of a radar-equipped Harrier was first mooted in a 1988 Marine Corps requirement for an upgraded AV-8 that could carry out attacks by both day and night, without regard for weather conditions. By combining the interest of the Navies of Spain and Italy, which also had a requirement for an aircraft that could carry out fleet defence and attack with the 'off the shelf' proven abilities of the APG65 radar system and the capabilities of FLIR-equipped Night Attack Harrier, an MoU (Memorandum of Understanding) was signed with the governments of Spain and Italy in 1990 jointly to fund radar integration and development for a new variant of the Harrier. McDonnell

⇧ A top view of the new nose profile of the II Plus showing the contours of the radome and FLIR fairing

⇧ Looking upwards at the nose of the II Plus, affording a great view of the underside contours of the radome

⇧ A pair of II Plus Harriers from VMA-223 'Bulldogs'. Note the chaff and flare dispensers on the upper rear fuselage

44　AIRData

⇧ 164560/CG of VMA-231. Note the chaff and flare dispensers are covered here

⇧ A II Plus from VMA-231 drops a pair of 'slick' bombs on target

⇧ A brace of 'Tigers' from VMA-542

⇧ A pair of Harrier from VMA-231

⇧ A pair of Harrier II Pluses taking on gas from a US Marines Hercules Tanker

⇧ With drop tanks and a Sidewinder training round, a Harrier II Plus come in to land

Douglas was thus awarded a contract on 3 December 1990, and the first Harrier II Plus, 164129, fitted with an APG-65Q4 radar took to the air on 22 September 1992, with test pilot Jackie Jackson at the helm.

With the concept having been proved, a second MoU was signed for the production of the Harrier II Plus in 1992, and manufacture began with aircraft 164548 which made its first flight on 17 March 1993, with the first deliveries to US squadron service beginning in June 1993. The US Marine Corps programme had called for all its remaining original AV-8B airframes to be converted to the II Plus standard in a concerted effort to standardise the Harrier fleet, and for twenty-seven new airframes to be produced. The reality of

⇧ Harrier II Plus aircraft from VMA-231 carrying the codes of HMM-263

⇧ Note how the aircraft ID numbers have been changed on the flap area

⇧ An 'Ace of Spades' Harrier comes in to land. Note the Rafael Litening II pod

46

⇧ A elongated view down the deck as a pair of Harriers prepare for launch

⇧ Harrier Power! An AV-8B II Plus converts from the hover to wing-borne flight – you can almost hear the noise

⇧ Note the Rafael Litening II pod here and the PGM practice round

⇧ Maintenance crews get to work on this Harrier

⇧ Full power on a rain soaked deck........

⇧ .....spray and steam everywhere........

⇧ .....as a VMA-231 Harrier gets airborne

the situation was that only seventy-three rebuilds were authorised from a total of 144 aircraft. However, the reworked AV-8Bs would have the benefit of the stronger, new-build Night Attack Standard fuselage, while retaining the original wings, tailfin, tailplane and undercarriage. The capability upgrade was a major advance even when measured against the Night Attack Harrier, giving the users a greater operational scope. The addition of several new and key systems also gave the jet a much wider envelope of 'missions for conditions'. For the US Marines, it is what they always desired: VSTOL with 'eyes', and for the first time the ability to operate their Harriers in all elements.

The Harrier II Plus retains all the avionics of the successful Night Attack Harrier, including the FLIR and upward and

⇧ Sitting on its engine power a Harrier II Plus slides across the deck for a landing

⇧ The pilot watches carefully as he prepares for launch

48 AIRData

⇧ Crews remove the tie-down chains for this Harrier as the 'Crash and Smash' team looks on

⇧ A Harrier II Plus recovers whilst another steams in behind

⇧ II Plus Noses!

⇧ Preparing for another trip from MCAS Yuma

⇧ A pair of Harriers wearing the codes of HMM-163 whilst aboard the USS Boxer

downward firing Goodyear AN/ALE-39 chaff/flare launchers scabbed to the upper and lower rear fuselage, and a lengthened RAM air intake at the base of the fin as well as the 100% LERX. The aircraft also has a new overwing antenna for the AN/APX-100 IFF set and the adoption of the RAF-type wing with four pylons per side. It also has the benefit of the powerful Rolls-Royce Pegasus F402-RR408 engine, the installation of the 100 per cent LERX, OPS receiver and provision for the AIM-120 AMRAAM missile. For the pilot it means the advantages of a laser disc-generated colour moving map, a Card File Computer System and a portable DSU (data storage unit). The DSU has taken away the need to feed flight information into the aircraft's computer while the pilot is sitting in the cockpit; this can now be done in the squadron's operations centre at the mission-planning stage. The pilots spend a great deal of time in the planning phase at the MOMS (maintenance operator and mapping station), which is a computer set to calculate timings, fuel, threat sector and navigational planning. The computer then provides the ingress and egress routes, required fuel, the positions of the known

⇧ A slightly different tail design for this 'Flying Nightmare' as it reflects its HMM-162 parent aboard ship

⇧ ....as a brace of thirsty Harrier II Plus aircraft formate.....

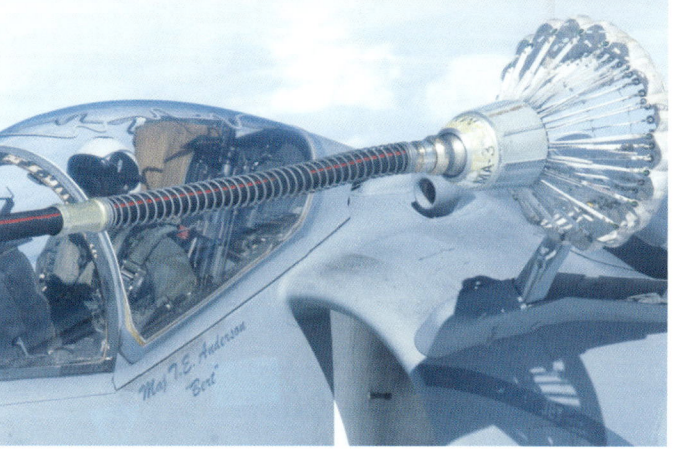

⇧ The tanker trails its hose and drouge....

⇧ ....the pilot plugs in.....

⇧ ....giving the aircraft some 'fresh legs'.....

⇧ ......thus extending its mission/patrol radius

⇧ A Harrier II Plus assigned to VX-9 'Vampires'

⇧ Caught in the late afternoon sun. Note the orange pod on the outer wing pylon

⇧ A excellent study of 165591/WF

⇧ Note the extremely 'sooty' gun pod here

⇧ Coming home in the late afternoon sun

threat corridors, weaponeering, moon or sun angles, communications, AN/APX100 IFF settings, flight 'cards' and load-outs.

The digital colour moving map is tied to the INS, and has given the Harrier II Plus a 'paperless cockpit' – no longer does the pilot have to carry the obligatory 'legful' of flight papers, as the aircraft's position is in constant view, in several scales from 1:1,000,000 down to 1:50,000, and relevant mission data, such as fuel, timings, threat data, navigation cues and 'reminders' all marked on the map display. The GEC Sensors FLIR is housed in an angular 'box' fairing in the centre of the nose section set back above the radome, and is just lower than the pilot's actual line of sight, thus giving him a far more realistic view forward than that provided by wing or fuselage mounted pods. The FLIR can be set to either white equals hot or black equals hot, depending on the pilot's choice, and is capable of piercing through all but the most severe rainstorms, which can degrade its performance. Its view forward can be projected

⇧ Harriers at sunset, a rest from the day's operations

⇧ Insignia of VMA-214 'Blacksheep'

⇧ Nose insignia of VMA-211 'Wake Island Avengers'

Special Markings

⇧ 164570 of VMA-231

⇧ 165397 of VMA-311

⇧ 165307 of VMA-542

⇧ 'The Great American Bulldogs'!

⇧ 163867 of VMAT-203

⇧ 165007 of VMA-211

⇧ 165006 of VMA-513

⇧ A Harrier II Plus taxies out from Kandahar Air Base for another patrol

onto the Harrier's wide-angle HUD or onto one of the two MPCDs, allowing the pilot to conduct 'day' tactics after dark. As a result of the introduction of the new nose shape, the Harrier's familiar 'yaw-vane' has been relocated to the right-hand side of the nose just in front of the windshield. Also included in the armoury of the Harrier II Plus is a Missile Approach Warning System (MAWS), the external 'eye' of which can be found in a faceted sensor beneath the aircraft's nose. This sensor detects 'flashes' and missile plumes by scanning in the ultraviolet and providing both a visual and an audible warning in the cockpit.

With their $20 million contract in hand, McDonnell

Seen during 'Operation Iraqi Freedom' a pair of aircraft from VMA-214 'Blacksheep'

⇧ A Harrier II Plus taxies out from Kandahar Air Base for another patrol

⇧ Note the full chaff and flare dispensers on this aircraft seen during 'Operation Iraqi Freedom'

⇧ A II Plus from VMA-214 awaits its next Gulf War II mission

⇧ A 'Flying Nightmare' Harrier is marshalled into position after a patrol over Iraq

⇧ Heading out for another armed patrol over Iraq

⇧ A Harrier II Plus armed and on patrol over Iraq

AIRData 55

⇧ Preparing to launch over Iraq

⇧ Late night repairs in Iraq

Douglas set about modifying AV-8B 164129 into a full-scale development airframe, as a precursor to an order for twenty-seven aircraft. It was flown ahead of schedule by 'Jackie' Jackson on 22 September 1992, and was passed to the Naval Air Weapons Centre for airframe and systems trials in early 1993 before being transferred to China Lake for radar evaluation. The second 'brand new II' was dispatched to VX-5 for further trials, while a third, 164548, was tested for carrier work before being delivered to its new masters VMA542 at Cherry Point in June 1993. No. 164129 also had its upper chaff/flare launchers faired over, did not carry the MAWS fitting and carried strakes instead of the gun pack.

Like its Night Attack cousins the Harrier II Plus has taken part in recent conflicts in Iraq and Afghanistan where it continues to operate at the time of writing. One of the most recent additions to the Harrier's armoury has been the Rafael Litening II pod, and the ability to designate PGM's and carry a greater range of munitions such as JDAM.

⇧ A Harrier pilot climbs aboard – note the internal steps

⇧ A 'Flying Nightmares' II Plus arrives for duty in Iraq

AV-8B Colour Profiles

⇩ To test the theories behind the AV-8B in a flight programme, two AV-8As were remanufactured as YAV-8B test aircraft. YAV-8B No.1, 158394 was completed on 1 September 1978. The aircraft wears a patriotic red, white and blue colour scheme with codes and Marines insignia in black, with a full colour 'stars and stripes' on the tail. The aircraft also has an instrumentation boom on the nose and the McDonnell Douglas logo on the outrigger wheel fairing

⇩ The first of the Full Scale Development aircraft YAV-8B 161396 made its first hover flight on 5 November 1981. The AV-8B was a totally changed aircraft compared with the YAV-8. The aircraft carries a grey lighter than the operational FS36099 Extra Dark Sea Grey, and Green FS34064 disruptive upper surfaces and Light Aircraft Grey FS36440 lower surfaces. All markings and insignia were black

⇩ AV-8B 162743/WH '09' of VMA-542 'Tigers'. The aircraft wears an overall wraparound camouflage scheme of Dark Sea Grey FS 36099 and Dark Green FS36064. All markings and insignia are black

⇩ AV-8B 162069/VL '000' of VMA-331 'Bumblebees' circa 1989. This aircraft wears an experimental low visibility finish of FS36118 over FS36440

⇩ AV-8B 162074/VL '07' of VMA-331 circa late 1989. The aircraft wears an overall wraparound camouflage scheme of Extra Dark Sea Grey FS 36099 and Dark Green FS36064. All markings and insignia are black

⇩ AV-8B 163668/WL '08' of VMA-311 'Tomcats' during Operation Desert Storm. The colours were mixed 'in theatre' and are near to FS36118 over FS36320

⇩ AV-8B 162964/CG '08' of VMA-231 'Ace of Spades' during Operation Desert Storm. The colours were mixed 'in theatre' and are near to FS36320 over FS36270

⇩ AV-8B Harrier carrying the tail code 'YS' and attached to HMM-162 aboard the USS Wasp. The aircraft carriers the low visibility Harrier Tactical Paint Scheme (HTPS) consisting of FS36118 upper surfaces, over FS36321 upper wings and fuselage sides and FS36320 lower surfaces. National insignia, stencils and squadron markings mirror the camouflage colours

⇩ AV-8B(NA) 162966/XE the Night Attack 'proof of concept' aircraft complete with nocturnal suite and fitted with a GEC Sensors FLIR mounted in front of the cockpit. The aircraft wears an overall wraparound camouflage scheme of Extra Dark Sea Grey FS 36099 and Dark Green FS36064. All markings and insignia are black, whilst the stylised nose artwork is in white

⇩ AV-8B(NA) Harrier of VMA-211 'Wake Island Avengers'. The aircraft carriers the low visibility Harrier Tactical Paint Scheme (HTPS) consisting of FS36118 upper surfaces, over FS36321 upper wings and fuselage sides and FS36320 lower surfaces. National insignia, stencils and squadron markings mirror the camouflage colours

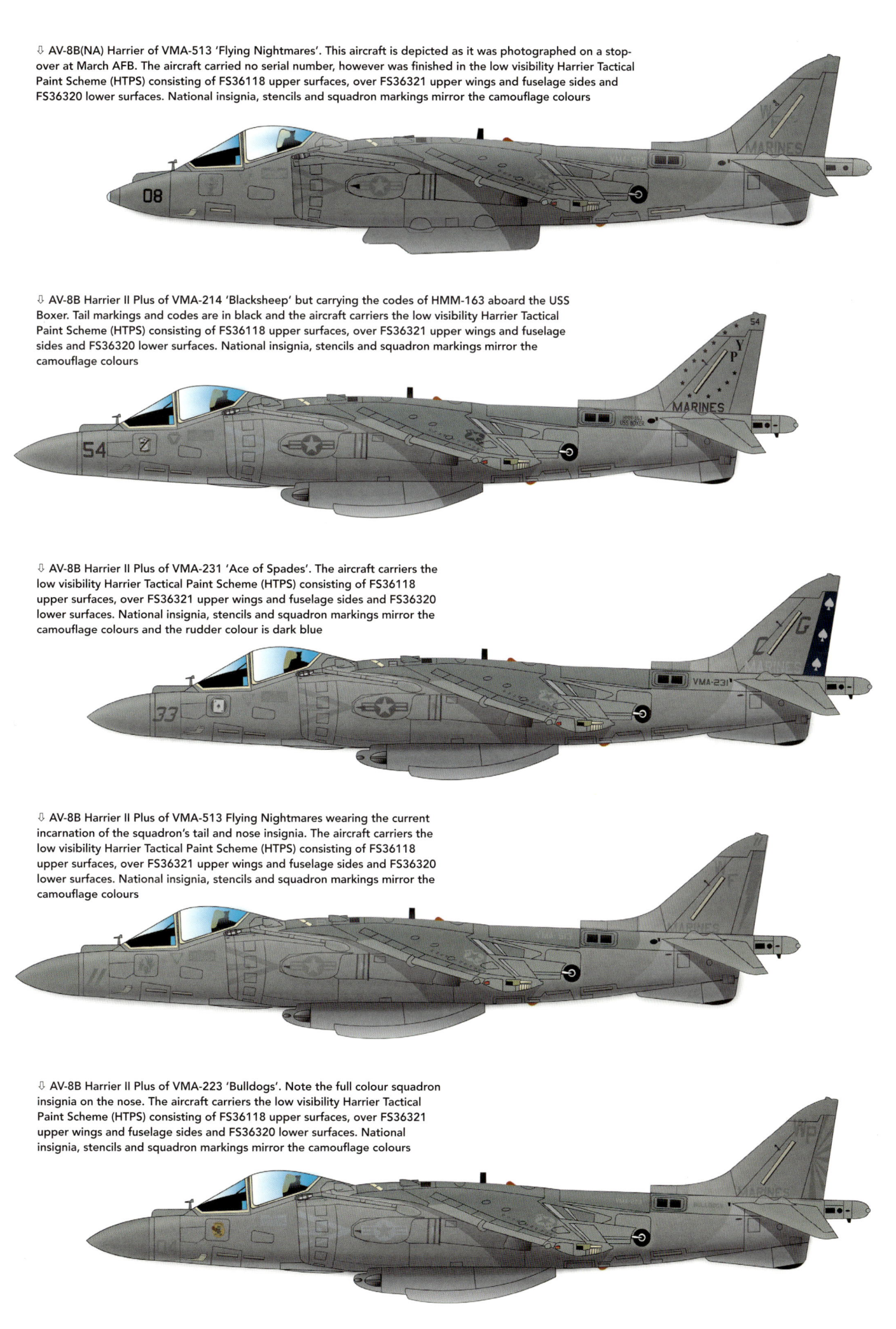

⇩ AV-8B(NA) Harrier of VMA-513 'Flying Nightmares'. This aircraft is depicted as it was photographed on a stop-over at March AFB. The aircraft carried no serial number, however was finished in the low visibility Harrier Tactical Paint Scheme (HTPS) consisting of FS36118 upper surfaces, over FS36321 upper wings and fuselage sides and FS36320 lower surfaces. National insignia, stencils and squadron markings mirror the camouflage colours

⇩ AV-8B Harrier II Plus of VMA-214 'Blacksheep' but carrying the codes of HMM-163 aboard the USS Boxer. Tail markings and codes are in black and the aircraft carriers the low visibility Harrier Tactical Paint Scheme (HTPS) consisting of FS36118 upper surfaces, over FS36321 upper wings and fuselage sides and FS36320 lower surfaces. National insignia, stencils and squadron markings mirror the camouflage colours

⇩ AV-8B Harrier II Plus of VMA-231 'Ace of Spades'. The aircraft carriers the low visibility Harrier Tactical Paint Scheme (HTPS) consisting of FS36118 upper surfaces, over FS36321 upper wings and fuselage sides and FS36320 lower surfaces. National insignia, stencils and squadron markings mirror the camouflage colours and the rudder colour is dark blue

⇩ AV-8B Harrier II Plus of VMA-513 Flying Nightmares wearing the current incarnation of the squadron's tail and nose insignia. The aircraft carriers the low visibility Harrier Tactical Paint Scheme (HTPS) consisting of FS36118 upper surfaces, over FS36321 upper wings and fuselage sides and FS36320 lower surfaces. National insignia, stencils and squadron markings mirror the camouflage colours

⇩ AV-8B Harrier II Plus of VMA-223 'Bulldogs'. Note the full colour squadron insignia on the nose. The aircraft carriers the low visibility Harrier Tactical Paint Scheme (HTPS) consisting of FS36118 upper surfaces, over FS36321 upper wings and fuselage sides and FS36320 lower surfaces. National insignia, stencils and squadron markings mirror the camouflage colours

Chapter 6
TAV-8B
Two-Seat Harrier Trainer

Due to the success of the TAV-8A, the US Marine Corps was not in favour of purchasing a dedicated Harrier II training vehicle, as they considered that the current system was more than adequate for their needs. In the AV-8B, trainee Harrier pilots first flew in the all-analogue TAV-8A cockpit then transitioned to the digital cockpit of the AV-8B. However, it soon became apparent that apart from the radical difference in the switchology, and the 'G' capabilities, the AV-8B had dramatically different handling characteristics to the AV-8A and it became clear that training for the 'Harrier II' needed a totally different aircraft to the first generation TAV-8A. The Marines therefore required a trainer that would faithfully replicate the abilities of this new breed of Harrier. Enter the TAV-8B.

The TAV-8B featured a lengthened forward fuselage (adding 3 ft 11in to the aircraft) housing stepped tandem cockpits for the student (front) and instructor (rear) and came fitted with full dual controls. The aircraft had a taller fin (17 in/43 cm) with a 75% LERX added to the leading edge, giving increased chord and area for improved directional stability. The environmental control system was also modified to cope with the demands of two cockpits. Unlike the TAV-8A, the new trainer did not have an extended tailcone, and as the TAV-8B was not designed to have an operational front-line role, it had only two external hardpoints, for the tactical weapons phase of the Harrier syllabus where these are used to carry practice munitions such as six Mk.76 Practice Bombs, LAU-68 rocket pods or two 250-gallon tanks. The underfuselage cannon armament is also available, but it is more usual to see the aircraft with the LID strakes fitted. The aircraft also carries two types of ejection seat, the Stencel SJU-13 in the front and the SJU-14 in the rear, the difference being that in the event of an ejection the front seat would diverge to the right and the rear seat to the left, ensuring that the occupants did not collide. The front cockpit is identical to that of the AV-8B, so that when the student eventually goes solo there is no difference (except the lack of an instructor in the back), and, like the AV-8B, does not posses a colour moving-map display, the track information being shown on a DDI, (digital display indicator). The instructor's rear suite contains full flight and engine controls, with further improvements including SAAHS and DECS-controlled engines.

TAV-8B 162747, the T-Bird development aircraft, took its

⇧ TAV-8B 162747, the T-Bird development aircraft

⇧ TAV-8B 162747/SD '626' of the Strike Aircraft Test Directorate at Patuxent River wearing the grey/green wraparound colour scheme

⇧ The side-hinged canopies are a classic feature of the two-seat Harrier

⇧ The larger forward fuselage accommodates both student and instructor and here you can see the LERX added to the leading edge of the wing

⇩ YAV-8B 162747/SD of the Strike Aircraft Test Directorate at Patuxent River. The aircraft wears the standard wraparound colours of Dark Sea Grey FS 36099 and Dark Green FS36064. All markings and insignia are black, with Day-Glo panels on the tail and wingtips

⇧ Canopies open waiting for their next students as a brace of TAV-8Bs sit on the flight line. The instructor's rear suite contains full flight and engine controls

⇧ The TAV-8B's larger front fuselage can be seen to good effect here

⇧ The TAV-8B has an increased tail fin to counterbalance the enlarged cockpit

61

⇧ The badge of VMAT-203 'The Hawks' the USMC's dedicated Harrier training unit

⇧ With the front canopy slightly 'cracked' open a TAV-8B taxies out

first flight in the hands of test pilot Jackie Jackson on the 21 October 1986, and he took an hour's sortie to pronounce that the new aircraft was going to be a success. The aircraft was painted in the standard USMC grey/green wraparound colours, with a test boom fitted to the nose. 162574 was about 1,400lb heavier than the equivalent squadron model owing to its test instrumentation and wiring, which for evaluation purposes were equated to a similar weight in ordnance. The first production example, 162963, arrived at the Marines' training unit VMAT-203 on 24 July 1987.

The task of producing pilots for the AV-8B falls on Marine Attack Training Squadron 203 (VMAT-203), 'The Hawks', based at MCAS Cherry Point. This unit bridges the gap between the 'rookie' flyer and the competent aviator with one of the seven prestige gun squadrons. The unit is unique in that it not only trains the pilots but also all the maintenance personnel as well. The 'Hawks' pioneered the training mission during the Marines Corps' transition from the `straight-liners' to the VSTOL regime and has the distinction of being the only Harrier training unit in the United States. VMAT-203's history may be traced back to 1927, and subsequently it has had various designations: VMT-1, VMT-203 and VMAT-203. VMT-1 began to train pilots on the TR-9J Cougar and the T-33 Shooting Star until 1967, when it received its first TA-4J Skyhawks, and was then redesignated VMT-203 in April 1968. May 1972 saw a further redesignation to VMAT-203, when it took on charge a mix of

⇧ The task of producing pilots for the AV-8B falls on Marine Attack Training Squadron 203 (VMAT-203), 'The Hawks', based at MCAS Cherry Point

⇧ As the TAV-8B was not designed to have an operational front-line role, it had only two external hardpoints

⇧ A 'factory fresh' looking TAV-8B showing its Harrier Tactical Paint Scheme (HTPS)

⇧ An unusual 'all over grey' Harrier – 163186 with FS36118 codes and markings

⇧ TAV-8B 163180 turns onto the runway for a training sortie

⇧ A TAV-8B 'peeps' out into the sunshine. Note the weathered appearance of the nose-cone

⇧ Note how the cockpits are separated by a windscreen

AIRData 63

⇧ The ubiquitous Harrier stepladder!

TA-4J and A4M Skyhawks, being tasked to train replacement pilots for fleet duty. April 1975 heralded the arrival of the AV-8A Harrier, and with it came the dedicated two-seater TAV-8A in October. The unit continued with these aircraft until the arrival of the AV-8B, when it had the dual role of training pilots on both the AV-8C and the B model until 1985 when its last 'C' pilot completed his course. From then its sole mission has been that of training on the AV-8B. VMAT-203 operates a mix of AV-8B and TAV-8Bs, and the previous tree-top level scheme of Dark Gull Grey, FS 32631, and European Green, FS 34092, camouflage has been replaced by the universally adopted Harrier Tactical Paint Scheme (HTPS) of Dark Sea Grey, FS 36118, applied to the top of the wings and fuselage, Dark Gull Grey, FS 36321, on the outer sections of the upper wings and fuselage sides, and Dark Ghost Grey, FS 36230 undersides.

⇧ A tri of trainers!

⇧ A TAV-8B 'buttoned-up' at an airshow event

Appendix I
Data 1

US Marine Corps Harrier Squadrons

VMA-211 'Wake Island Avengers'
VMA-211 can trace its lineage to January 1 1937 when Marine Fighting Squadron 4 (VF-4M) was activated at Naval Air Station San Diego, California. In September 1987, the squadron celebrated an aviation milestone when it passed 30 years of flying the McDonnell Douglas A-4 Skyhawk. After successfully completing the last overseas deployment with the type in 1989 VMA-211 began preparations for transition to the AV-8B Night Attack Harrier beginning operations in June of that year. In September 2000, the squadron began introduction of the latest Harrier variant, the AV-8B II Plus, soon fielding a complement of both radar and Night Attack Harriers.

VMA-214 'Black Sheep'
Marine Fighter Squadron 214 was originally commissioned on July 1, 1942, at Marine Corps Air Station Ewa, on the Island of Oahu. Initially called the 'Swashbucklers', the squadron is best known as the 'Black Sheep' of World War II fame and for one of its commanding officers, Colonel Gregory 'Pappy' Boyington. In 1989 the Black Sheep introduced the 'Night Attack' Harrier aircraft to the Marine Corps and continues its mission in both Iraq and Afghanistan.

VMA-223 'Bulldogs'
Marine Fighter Squadron 223 (VMF-223) was commissioned on May 1, 1942 at Marine Corps Air Station Ewa, Oahu, Hawaii on the Brewster F2A Buffalo. In May 1975, the squadron received the new A-4M Skyhawk aircraft which they flew until October 1987 when VMA-223 transitioned to the AV-8B Harrier. VMA-223 deployed to Iraq late in the summer of 2005 in support of Operation Iraqi Freedom and during a combat mission over Iraq on February 10, 2006 the squadron surpassed the 60,000 mishap-free hours mark.

VMA-231 'Ace of Spades'
VMA-231 began as the 1st Division, Squadron 1 on February 8 1919 - a unit that emerged from the Northern Bombing Group of Northern France in 1918. VMA-231 was reactivated on May 15, 1973, and the Marine Corps' oldest squadron became the Corps newest, flying the AV-8A Harrier, later converting to the AV-8B.

VMA-311 'Tomcats'
Born immediately following the Japanese attack on Pearl Harbour, Marine Fighting Squadron 311 (VMF-311) was first commissioned on 1 December 1942, assigned to the 3rd Marine Aircraft Wing and headquartered at MCAS Cherry Point. In 1988 VMA-311 received its first AV-8B Harrier and on August 11, 1990, after the Iraqi invasion of Kuwait, VMA-311 deployed in support of Operation Desert Shield. On January 15, 2003, the Marines of VMA-311 deployed to the Northern Persian Gulf as part of Amphibious Task Force West. On March 21, 2003, almost 59 years to the day after VMF-311's first combat sortie in World War II, the Tomcats flew their first combat sortie of Operation Iraqi Freedom.

VMA-331 'Bumblebees'
Marine Scout Bomber Squadron 331 (VMSB-331) was formed on January 1, 1943 at Marine Corps Air Station Cherry Point, North Carolina. On January 25, 1985 VMA-331 became the first fully operational AV-8B unit in Marine Corps service. The squadron deployed on the USS Nassau (LHA-4) to the Persian Gulf and eventually flew 243 sorties dropping 256 tons of ordnance and became the first Marine Attack Squadron to conduct combat operations from a Landing Helicopter Assault ship. The unit left the Gulf on 10 March 1991 and was subsequently deactivated on 30 September 1992.

VMA-513 'Flying Nightmares'
Marine Attack Squadron 513 was first commissioned as VMF-513 on February 15 1944 at Marine Corps Auxiliary Field Oak Grove, North Carolina, flying the Grumman F6F Hellcat. Moving to MCAS Cherry Point, the squadron flew the F-4B Phantom until June 30, 1970, when it was recommissioned, awaiting delivery of the first AV-8A Harrier on April 16 1971 and re-designated VMA-513. In February 1991, VMA-513 deployed for Desert Shield and Desert Storm employing its new AV-8Bs in support of the 15th Marine Expeditionary Unit, and today continue its mission in both Iraq and Afghanistan.

VMA-542 'Tigers'

Marine Attack Squadron 542 was initially commissioned as Marine Night Fighter Squadron 542 (VMF(N)-542) on March 6, 1944, at Marine Corps Air Station Cherry Point, North Carolina flying the F6F Hellcat. On January 12, 1972 the squadron received the designation of Marine Attack Squadron (VMA) 542 and were assigned the new AV-8A Harrier. The Tigers were relocated to MCAS Cherry Point, North Carolina in August 1974 and April 1986 saw the end of the AV-8A and C models as the Tigers transitioned to the AV-8B. In August 1990, the Tigers deployed to the Bahrain in support of Operation Desert Shield before moving to King Abdul Aziz Naval Base during Desert Storm. They continue their mission in both Iraq and Afghanistan.

VMAT-203 'The Hawks'

Marine Attack Training Squadron 203 dates back to 1947 when as VMT-1 it began as an independent squadron and shortly thereafter became part of Marine Training Group 20. In May 1972, the squadron was redesignated VMAT-203 with a new mix A-4M, and TA-4J aircraft and tasked with training replacement aircrews. The arrival V/STOL heralded another era for VMAT-203 as the Skyhawks were retired and VMAT-203 became the AV-8A/C training squadron. In December 1983, the first was delivered, and until March 1985, VMAT-203 was assigned the dual missions of training both AV-8A/C pilot and AV-8B replacement aircrews. Having trained its last AV-8A/C pilot in March 1985, VMAT-203's exclusive mission then became the training of AV-8B aircrews and maintenance personnel.

Appendix II
AV-8B Data

Data	Harrier II Plus	AV-8B(NA) Night Attack	iAV-8B
Aircraft Length (feet)	47.75	46.33	46.33
Aircraft Height (feet)	11.66	11.66	11.66
Aircraft Wingspan (feet)	30.35	30.35	30.35
Operating Weight Empty (pounds)	14,912	13,968	13,705
Maximum Vertical Takeoff Weight (pounds)	20,752	20,752	19,185
Maximum Short Takeoff Weight (pounds)	32,000	32,000	31,000
Internal Fuel Weight (pounds)	7,762	7,762	7,762
Maximum External Fuel Weight (pounds)	8,073	8,073	8,073